THE DARKNESS
BEFORE LIGHT

Turning Despair into Creative Inspiration

Cecilia Beltran

First printing, March 2013

ISBN-13: 978-1477552391

ISBN-10: 1477552391

BISAC: Psychology/Self-help

Printed in the United States of America

To my two great lights:

my daughter, Sophia,

and my husband, Ronnie

Acknowledgements

The Darkness Before Light grew out of an e-mail exchange with my good friend, Florence Thomas, an author (*The Mistake*) I met while I was living in Prague. I had been writing another book for seven years and grappling with the complexity of the topic I had chosen. Florence encouraged me to do a short book about a simple topic that would be around twenty pages long.

The book grew from twenty pages to over one hundred. It bears some of the research I've done for the other book. I am very pleased with how it turned out. I owe Florence greatly for the encouragement.

Marc Oromaner, the author of *The Myth of Lost*, gave a comprehensive critique of this book in the early stages. I am deeply grateful for his help. I thank Professor Jorge Cabrales, an educator and a practicing psychotherapist in New York who organized the *Jung Transpersonal Group* I participate in, for reading my manuscript and giving his valuable opinion. I thank Dr. Morrin Bass of the *New York Awareness Center*, for her review of my work and for the enriching conversations. I also thank Monica Angelucci, my mentor in yoga, for lending me her gems.

I thank Stephen Gerringer, Community Relations Head for the Joseph Campbell Foundation,for allowing me to use Joseph Campbell's quotes.

To Dr. Dean Simonton, PhD, distinguished professor of the Psychology Department of the University of California, my sincere thanks for his permission to use quotes from his article in the Scientific American Mind.

To Benedict Carey, science reporter for the New

York Times, my sincere appreciation for allowing me to use excerpts of his work on James Hillman.

I also would like to thank Samantha Sotto, best-selling author of *Before Ever After*, for her beautiful review and for her generous encouragement.

I also thank Arnold Barrera, my dear friend, mentor in shamanism and esoteric studies. He opened my eyes. I thank Reg Ofrin, sensei and beloved ally, for introducing me to eastern philosophy and macrobiotics. Much of what he has taught me is the foundation of this book. To fellow author, Regina Khan, one of my best friends, I also give my thanks for her insightful critique and editing.

To my brilliant sisters: Tin Sanchez, for her creative expertise, the few minutes of feedback was worth a thousand; and Gigi Victoriano, for our shared fascination for Greek mythology. Also, I thank my dear friends Charlie and Maria Hayon, for the time they took reading my manuscript, for the intellect and sincerity they shared.

I also want to say "thank you" to my mother for banishing television despite protests and instead giving us a large allowance for books growing up; and to my husband, Ronnie Beltran, for his insistence on excellence that is founded on his unwavering faith in my abilities. (Hera smiles at you)

-Cecilia Beltran

CONTENTS

❦

Prologue

—≈—

It felt like hollowness in my stomach. There was a screaming in my head. I wanted to end the pain that was nagging at the base of my chest. I looked at the open window and contemplated throwing myself out. The night seemed darker than most nights. I stared at the darkness. The aloof pinpricks of light coming from the jagged skyline of Bangkok flickered in the distance.

In the lot below, a live elephant was sleeping. It had trampled on the grass around it. Some say elephants never forget. I wondered if it had some memories it wished would just go away. I thought, dispassionately, how interesting it would be to die staring at that exotic animal face to face like it was my memories that killed me. I began to climb out the window and put my right leg out, testing how far I would really go. My lips thinned at the mean intent.

My heart did not even skip a beat. I tilted my head to the side wondering if I could shed the pain with my body. I let the idea dance in my mind. I knew I would not really jump but wished that I would. Then, I heard the door click. It was my husband coming home late from work. I didn't want to face him. I was ashamed of my own despair and angry that he didn't know it was there. I pulled my leg back in, climbed into bed, and pretended to sleep. Sleep crept slowly. It came with nightmares of being trapped in a haunted house. The next morning, I woke up, called Bumrungrad Hospital, and scheduled a visit to a psychologist.

He could have been a Buddhist monk. He had a quiet and patient air about him. His shaved head and the slight smile on his face were soothing. The psychologist spoke in heavily accented English. He listened to the reasons I had for seeking his help, urging me, with short questions, to go on. As I listened to myself talk about why I contemplated throwing myself out the window the night before, I began to understand. The reasons were irrelevant. I was depressed, and the real cause was unknown to me. I recognized that all the things I complained about—though legitimately saddening—did not quite explain why I had thought of ending my life the night before.

The source of my pain was inside. It was hiding in my mind behind the images of people that I blamed for my despair.

In a measured tone, the psychologist finally said, "Perhaps you are bored."

"Excuse me?"

"Are you bored?"

I was taken aback. I never thought I was bored. It seemed a very shallow reason to want to end my life. But it dawned on me that boredom was a symptom of a larger affliction. I had lost interest in my own life. I took on a new role when I married my husband. As the self-appointed provider, his career path took precedence over mine. I had willingly set aside my own dreams so that we could be together. I had retired from living my life in order to be in his.

People who go into actual retirement or lose their jobs unexpectedly usually fall into depression. A title or a label helps to anchor them to a sense of self, even if they don't know who that person really is.

I recognize that the sudden change of

pace was a consequence of the particular knot I had tied. I had willingly decided to follow him wherever he went—unaware that it meant leaving myself behind. I was unprepared for that realization. Everyone told me I was lucky. I didn't realize that I was no longer someone I know. I was just someone's wife—the wife of a roaming workaholic. I assumed that marrying my charming and gracious husband was a cure to this feeling of being alone. I did not know it then. I realized later that loneliness had more to do with being disconnected with oneself rather than not having meaningful connections with others.

Living in a strange country with no one to talk to and with nothing particularly important to do highlighted what I failed to observe about myself when I was busy with work. I had suddenly been thrust into a world where I could not hide behind labels or associations that I had gathered along the way. I even lost my name. I now introduced myself by another name: the name of my husband.

That was perhaps what the trip to the psychologist's clinic had done for me. He had pointed out that the source of my pain was that I had lost interest in myself. That was what he meant by being bored. I then had a thought that perhaps this hollow space where my old self used to be planted may be the cup of my fulfillment. In order to fill the feeling of emptiness that I had, I needed to find out the dimensions of the negative space that I carved out of me by the choices I had made.

I left the psychologist's office and never went back. What I had shared with him was enough to make me aware of where to go next. I decided to find my way back to finding a new purpose that was now applicable to my new life. I picked up my camera and roamed around the countryside in search of a sense of self that I had lost by voluntarily living my new husband's life and dreams. I took pictures of the things that drew my interest. I drove many hours alone in a 4x4, passing through mountains that were reminiscent of Chinese paintings. I was suddenly aware of just how deeply I hungered for meaning. I realized that all this time my life was being spent on things I did not truly care about. I took more and more pictures, and later on, I would stare and wonder why I was drawn to take them. I had taken the life of an explorer: roaming the Thai countryside like I roamed my own soul.

One day, outside my apartment building in Bangkok, I saw a Buddhist monk walk into a small street lined with shanties a few paces from my apartment. The tiny houses were hidden behind a wall that separated the posh expatriate community across the street. Born and raised Catholic, I thought it was an exotic sight. The monk's orange robe was a contrast to the greyness of the makeshift homes. I was drawn to follow the enigmatic figure while clutching my camera in my hand and waiting for a moment to capture the scene. He turned to a narrow path where bare-bottomed children were running around unsupervised, their noses dripping with phlegm. They were not miserable. In fact, they seemed happy. I followed the monk farther in. After another turn, I was surprised to find that in the middle of all the chaos—stolen planks of wood, rusting metal, and broken flower pots—was a magnificent *wat* (a Buddhist temple). It rose in the middle of the street like a lotus amid a swamp filled with flies and frogs. I followed the monk inside.

A man by the gate instructed me to remove my shoes. I went inside the pristine surroundings. My inexperienced feet tingled with the heat of the marble floor. Chimes were ringing from the mild breeze. A few meters away, the monk's robes flew gently in the wind.

I peered inside the unfamiliar world and saw a gigantic golden Buddha peacefully raising his one hand in blessing while the other one begged. I thought it was a curious gesture. Then I understood it. One hand blesses while the other one begs! I thought the gesture was a powerful metaphor for what it meant to be alive—to truly live. I used to think that happiness came from merely receiving all that I yearned for. I realized from gazing at the foreign image of the Buddha before me that I was not a jar to be filled but a pipe through which divine energy flows. I stared at the image and began to feel myself crying—perhaps from a kind of relief. It was like I had suddenly found a drink of water in barren land after a long thirst.

I came home that day with a profound understanding of the hole I felt inside me. I roamed far away and spent hours each day in search of meaning, and I found it, quite poetically, right in front of my doorstep. It had been waiting for me. I found that fate had set up the events that would make me aware of the life purpose that I had unknowingly been waiting for desperately.

The shape of the suffering I felt and the feelings of lack had all along been the negative space of my highest aspiration. It was calling out to me. The hole was a mold of what I needed to create in my life in order to finally be filled where it counts.

Perhaps it's the same for all of us. It was this insight that gave me the determination to take on the journey of self-awareness. I spent most of the succeeding years poring through ancient books, being led from one esoteric tradition to another until I finally grasped in full clarity the value of the gem I found that day. Underneath all religious thought, I learned, was a simple truth—that we are all creators who are designed to generate light in the darkness.

It is how we could become empowered

and not mere creations of our environment reacting to whatever life throws at us and never really knowing internal rest. I found myself believing that we are patterned against the very design that created us. We have always been meant to explode with light, and with this light, our universe is created anew.

It has not been an easy path attempting to share this breakthrough with others. Many people ask for external assurances that what I share with them can be trusted. Most people recoil at receiving instruction from someone they deem to be ordinary like themselves, as they put it. Those who have not embraced the ordinary in them as part of what makes them divine sometimes have illusions that a million dollars more or an advanced degree will make their life lessons more valuable. The truth is, we all are holding on to gems that may be valuable to someone else. We are all light bearers in our own right.

For a while, I believed I needed to acquire that title in order to share what I have learned seeking my own salvation from a dark time in my life. But it only derailed me more. Would I really need to spend thousands of dollars and more years in an institution to get the permission to speak about what saved me from despair? I didn't want the small lamp of hope that I found unexpectedly in that obscure street in Bangkok to die out without being passed on to others who may be inspired by it just because I deemed myself unworthy to be heard.

It seemed like a horrible vanity to demand being believed—to ram my credibility down other people's throats as if I don't find myself credible. I instead decided to forego the vanity and just offer what I have learned, as it is, and as I am now. I had received it as a gift: a gift that I was meant to give away to others. My life lessons were not mine to keep. This was the only way for me to grow further.

A documentary on PBS by the filmmaker David Grubin about the life of the Buddha gave me some validation that I had made the right choice. Once again, the Buddha's life showed me the way forward. His journey of enlightenment explained the final stages of my own awakening.

I will quote the part of the film that resonated the courage I felt when I decided to write this book:

"As he set off to share what he had learned, he met a wandering ascetic. 'Who is your guru?' the ascetic asked him. The Buddha said he had no guru, that he had attained enlightenment on his own. 'It may be so,' the ascetic said, and walked away. On his first attempt to teach, the Buddha had failed."

- (Venerable Metteyya Sakyaputta)

"Buddha meets someone who doesn't see anything special about him, because the awakened Buddha doesn't look any different from anybody else. He is ordinary. Buddhism is not about being special. Buddhism is about being ordinary. And it is not about the continual exudation of bliss. It is about walking a normal human life with normal human beings, doing normal human things. And this reminds you that you yourself might be a Buddha. At this moment, the person you're looking at might be one. It's an interesting practice. Just each person you see as you walk down the street: 'Buddha? Buddha? Buddha?'"

- (Jane Hirshfield)

Now that I conduct workshops on creative empowerment in New York, I make it a point to say that I can only reach those who have already learned their own truths. Teachers serve as a kind of lens through which a student perceives what is already dawning within him. So whatever it is a teacher shares, it can only be received by those who are already beginning to crave for it.

The path out of darkness is an individual one bearing its own unique twists and obstacles. But, it is also a universal journey borne from the common experience of being human.

14

There are those that suffered the dark night of the soul and managed to extract a great light from its belly. They transformed the way we see the world. They were once ordinary people too, suffering a commonplace despair. But we call them luminaries now. Their truths have continued to shape ours.

While their physical bodies had not survived the darkness, the light they found there still lived on. They gave us more profound ways of understanding ourselves and the world we live in.

This book is my humble offering. It is a small lamp that may shed light on the shape of that darkness you feel inside you. It is my hope that my truth and yours will meet in your heart so that they may become a glimmer of light. May that light grow bright, and may it light the way of others too.

Chapter One

—꜄꜃—

Unmasking the Daemon

"...happiness at its ancient source means eudemonia,

or a well-pleased daemon..."

—James Hillman, *The Soul's Code*

.

My sister woke up screaming one night from a nightmare. I rushed to her bedside and tried to calm her down. She was a teenager who had just experienced her first broken heart. A boy from a neighboring school had suddenly lost interest in her, and she was devastated—as any young person would be. She had cried herself to sleep the night before only to awaken like this—terrified.

"There were three dark shadows with curly hair and red eyes that swallowed me!" she cried out as she clutched the sleeve of my nightdress.

"Shhh…it's just a dream; it's over now," I said, trying to calm her panic. But it was not over. This dream marked the beginning of a chronic depression that would haunt her until her adult years.

Years later, when I began conducting Third Eye Awakening Workshops in New York, I came across a number of people who had also dreamt of three shadows with red eyes overpowering them at the onset of their depression. Most of them believed the shadowy figures were demonic forces.

What is interesting about these people is that they seemed to possess uncommon talent or even extraordinary kindness. A few enjoyed some amount of fame in their field, or they are involved in humanitarian projects.

I am fortunate to have the friendship of a very wise Hermetic Shaman who mentored me in the esoteric arts. He once said that those that are gifted are often attacked by dark entities. "They feed on their light." He had said this to me one afternoon in Manila over *bibinkas* (a kind of pancakes made of rice flour and coconut milk) and strong Filipino coffee. At the time, I took it at face value, believing that he meant actual demonic spirits lurking in the air eating up holiness from people's auras. I did not clarify, because he was always evasive about such things and always mumbling about readiness.

I realized later on that whenever my shaman friend spoke like this, he was speaking in symbols. It was his most time-efficient way to transfer to me his knowledge. It also added the extra precaution that I would only be able to decode it when I had done the work necessary to understand it.

One night, I called him to ask about a book we had talked about in one of our long discussions. He was drunk that night and was mumbling something strange to me.

"I have spoken to the Three [demons] and they said that they will give it to me," he said in slurred speech. While the polite thing to do would have been to call him at another time, curiosity got the better of me, and I pressed on.

"Give you what?" I asked, ignoring the strange detail that he had just claimed to be speaking to demons.

"The secret name," he whispered.

"Of what?"

"Of God," he said as if it were something that was obvious. I then decided that the conversation was becoming creepier than I was ready for. I told him to get some sleep, and I said good night.

At the time, I did not understand what he said and admittedly questioned his sanity. It was only when I read the work of James Hillman, author of *The Soul's Code*, that I understood what he was trying to tell me. The connection between demons and divine creative power has long been the theme of many myths. Demons in world mythology had always been threshold guardians of something dangerous and powerful. They would never give it willingly, though, without a test or a risk to the hero's soul. My shaman friend (and mentor) was speaking of being at the cusp of uncovering a secret power hidden in the things that torment him about himself. All three aspects of the Self, (the id, the ego and superego) had "agreed" to reveal the true countenance of his shadow self and release him from confusion.

The Name

Names of God in Jewish Mysticism seem to be about transcendent power. One example is The Name, or *Hashem*, as Jewish people call It. Christians phonetically sound it out as Yahweh, although how it is really pronounced is unknown:

יהוה

Christians even casually refer to The Name as the Old Testament God. The Jewish people, on the other hand, believe it is ineffable—meaning it cannot be uttered or expressed.

After studying the Hebrew letters and their meaning in Jewish mystical thought, I suspected why The Name bears a symbolic code. I concluded that it must be a divine act that has an equivalent human act of consciousness. *YHVH* after all, begins with a *yud*, the Hebrew "Y." Yud is a word and ideogram that depicts action.

YaHWeH, when read in ancient Semitic ideograms (pictographs that describe ideas), can be read as:

[The] act *(Y)* of beholding *(H)*

expands *(V)* beholding *(H).*

Rabbinical Hebrew is a tradition of deciphering the meaning of a Hebrew word through the letters it contains. For example, the Hebrew word for water, *mayim,* is made of the following symbols: water *(M)* and act *(Y).* So the Hebrew letters in the word *mayim* describe water as *water acting [as] water.* It is fluid and flowing, not vapor or ice.

The Name's ideograms surprised me in their description of what is believed to be *the most powerful name of God.* I correlate it to what is known in physics today as the "observer effect" In quantum theory, the observer effect is used to explain the idea that "there is no phenomenon until it is observed."[1] This implies that the act of observing something is what activates Its expansion or manifestation. Otherwise, the thing remains in an undetermined state—neither force nor matter. New Age sages say it more plainly: "Whatever you focus on, expands."

This name of God, in that light, is indeed the most powerful *and* most dangerous of all. The insight must be handled with caution. Because if it so, then it implies that the way you look at reality creates it.

Does this mean that when you look at despair as an evil affliction that will be what it is? Our culture regards despair as a malady, but it was not always the case. Despair, before it became clinical depression was once attributed to being haunted by demons.

[1] Alex Paterson, "The Observer Effect," (March 2008):
http//www.vision.net.au/~apaterson/science/observer_effect.htm.

In most myths, demons threaten, torture, or seduce the hero when they are at the cusp of attaining their victory. In the case of Buddha, it was a demon called Mara that ripened the enlightenment of Siddhartha beneath the Bodhi tree.

"Even if you find out the truth, who do you think will ever believe you? What right do you have to claim the throne of enlightenment?" Mara had said. To which the Buddha replied, "The earth is my witness...," and he touched the earth he sat on, signifying that his authority came from the natural world. I understand it this way: the stirrings of the human soul mirror that of the earth. The dawning of light from darkness, the seed's escape from the dark earth that buried it, and lastly, the body's own cycles of sleep and wakefulness all point to a pattern that can be observed everywhere. We also experience the virtual movements of night and day in our souls. It is the key to transcendence. Like the earth, we are moved by the turning of an internal wheel of light and darkness. It is the acknowledgement that these forces flow through us that make us able to navigate the seasons of our own psyche and master it.

Despite the mean activities of the Greek goddess Hera, she lent her name to the word *hero*. It is because *her* challenges push the half-mortal into heroic feats that he is eventually worthy of Mount Olympus.

Demons are distorted forces of the psyche that challenge the birthing of one's life purpose. James Hillman, author of *The Soul's Code*, makes a case that the demon is the rejected daemon insisting to come into the world all at once, disrespecting the cycles of darkness and light that creates time. Writing about Hillman's passing in an article for *The New York Times* (October, 2011), Benedict Carey reflects that in Hillman's eyes,

"...a person's demons really were demons, and the best course was to accept and understand them. To try to banish them, he said, was only to ask for more trouble. He might advise a parent trying to manage, say, a mentally troubled son to begin by "stop trying to change him."" [2]

So, that made me think that the daemon is a neutral force. Its benevolence or malevolence is entirely dependent on the way we perceive them.

---

[2] Benedict Carey, James Hillman, 85 Therapist in Men's Movement, Dies, The New York Times, Oct. 28, 2011

Aladdin's Genius

The metaphoric language in the story of Aladdin is clever in its portrayal of the neutrality of this force in the psyche.

The first time I came across the story of Aladdin was from a book that my father brought home when I was a child. *The Arabian Nights Entertainment* contained a compilation of Arabic folktales that was translated into English in the 1600s.

The story tells of the adventures of Aladdin. Unlike the popular version, Aladdin was not the Arabic version of Robin Hood. He was an irresponsible young man who thieved and lived aimlessly. Thieving in myth often points to an impending hero's distorted potentiality—until a purpose is introduced.

One day, an evil magician posing as a lost relative asked him to fetch a lamp from a dark cave that contained treasures. When Aladdin refused to give the magician the lamp for fear of being tricked, the magician closed the opening of the cave in anger. He escaped through the help of a genie. Aladdin later became a very wealthy man who won the sultan's daughter's hand in marriage.

Through the help of two genies, Aladdin's impossible wishes came true. But the two genies had different powers. The genie of the ring brought him out of the cave and helped him survive. It was the genie of the lamp that helped him reclaim his lost power and later, forever banish the evil magician that sought to steal it from him. The story portrayed the genie of the lamp as an entity that would go against you if you did not possess the lamp where it resided.

The word genie itself comes from an

Arabic word that means "the hidden." [3] It shares the same root as the word *mad*, which is defined as "one whose intellect is hidden."

Myth is largely symbolic of events in human consciousness. Aladdin's lamp, for me, symbolizes our hidden power—our own undiscovered creative genius that more often than not suddenly manifests after the psyche is threatened by a dark force.

This excerpt is the point when Aladdin lost his newfound power to a dark magician— an external negative influence that made it necessary for Aladdin to discover a more powerful ally within.

> "For three days [Aladdin] wandered about like a madman, asking everyone what had become of his palace, but they only laughed and pitied him. He came to the banks of a river, and knelt down to say his prayers before throwing himself in. In

[3] Hans Wehr, *Dictionary of Modern Written Arabic, 4th ed.* (Urbana: Spoken Language Services, 1994), 164.

so doing he rubbed the magic ring he still wore.

The genie he had seen in the cave appeared, and asked his will.

'Save my life, genie,' said Aladdin, 'and bring my palace back.'

'That is not in my power,' said the genie; 'I am only the slave of the ring; you must ask the slave of the lamp.'"[4]

What this means is that the task exceeds Aladdin's natural power to control his environment. Rings represent this power. Rings are also indicative of being bound or enslaved by the same power, the power of conscious will. The task requires a stroke of brilliance and creativity that has nothing to do with will. In place of will, there should be trust. A lamp symbolizes the creative consciousness necessary

---

[4] Edited by Andrew Lang, *The Blue Fairy Book*, Longman's Green &Co. New York,1889

to produce miracles.[5]

It is interesting to me that the word *genius* was derived from the same root as *genie*. Islamic belief says that genies are creatures of free will, made "with smokeless fire by Allah." It seems to me to be referring to passion, the fire of divine inspiration. It is divine because it is larger than a mere human inspiration, and its source is not within the walls of the individual's life experiences. It erupts from nowhere and it transcends the status quo.

In the story of Aladdin, the genie is trapped inside an old lamp, buried with treasure. When the genie is being summoned, Aladdin pulls the lamp out from his breast. This implies that this metaphorical lamp is taken from the heart—our source of truth. Authenticity plays a role in summoning the genie. A person's true passion is a shining inner

---

[5] A.Ronnberg and K. Martin, *The Book of Symbols, Reflections on Archetypal Images* Cologne, Germany, TASCHEN, 2010, 546, 580.

source of energy that illuminates the dark night of the soul and transforms it into a powerful ally.

The Daemon's Disguise

A "daemon," according to the Greeks, is a spirit that takes over and initiates an ordinary human being into a genius. The ancient Greeks believed that daemons are responsible for the presence of talent. Said to be the army of Zeus, the Greek god of thunder, daemons bestow greatness to the worthy mortal. Zeus symbolizes creative inspiration; Daemons are guardians of that inspiration. I have come to understand that even gods and goddesses in myths are actually symbolic of forces of the human psyche. The stories expose abstract concepts and their connections to each other using the lens of human experiences and relationships.

Creative inspiration (Zeus) seeds the mortal (the ordinary) and fathers heroic urges (Heracles, Hero), which are tested by creative inspiration's other half—jealousy, the gateway to marriage with potential (Hera). Beauty, also love (Aphrodite), is married to the deformed and rejected (Hephaestus) but has shameful entanglements with hate (Ares). Wisdom (Athena) emerged from creative inspiration (Zeus) fully formed.

When you look at what the gods rule, it is easier to digest what they stand for. They are not merely entertaining stories about powerful deities that act like children. The Greek myths are psychic themes. They are narratives of the conflicts and triumphs of the human soul and how they mirror the natural world.

Metaphors for our creative passions before they take a recognizable form, the daemons of Zeus steer us to unexpected directions that lead us to our true path. They are the unconscious stirrings inside us that make us suddenly sign up for a lesson or even take a serendipitous "wrong turn" where we will meet our master teacher.

Some people believe that daemons are spirit guides that lead us to our destiny. But I believe the daemon is a psychic force that reveals a person's special talent. It does not reside outside of us, nor completely generated by us. It is a force in between that connects us, as individuals, to the whole. We are born with this force, but it does not serve us. Rather, we are here to become its gateway into the world.

Talent is attributed to one that possesses an above average aptitude for a certain skill. However, talent is not skill. You do not birth talent by practicing the skill. It becomes evident because of skill, yes; but its source is more primal. It is an insatiable desire to answer a calling from within or to embody an idea (in the case of dancing or acting). Talent is a manifestation of a more vital force of life—passion.

When a person's talent inspires the world, the ability to express that talent collectively expands. Someone who sings a song strikingly inspires others to access emotions that could not have been generated on their own. Most often, those who listen are inspired to sing too. The sharing of talent fertilizes collective ability and learning. Passion may be the author of memes that accelerate evolution. It is what is needed to make life learn and grow.

Since the beginning, Life is connected from one generation to the next as well as from species to species in one pursuit. This collective pursuit is to improve not only how to survive or the quality of life itself; it's passionate about pushing consciousness forward.

Life is preoccupied with remembering what it knows and expanding that knowledge. And it does so by keeping the chain of life going. Each life-form that dies, I feel, is like a book that is lost in life's library.

Each living person unconsciously plays a

vital role in the fulfillment of this universal pursuit. We are all part of a long train of thought that perhaps began when the simplest notion of moving toward the food source crossed life's mind. I believe that the first eukaryotic cells were conscious. These founding fathers of life were at least aware that they could move away from what would kill them or go toward what would feed them.

Today we have gone beyond the search for food and safety. We are now in pursuit of answers to existential questions. Where did we come from, and why are we here? We are trying to collectively become aware of why we began to embark on the journey of living in the first place.

Whatever it is that we are drawn to, we must fulfill a role in that collective mission. A person pursuing his or her own passion—whether it is to paint masterpieces or collect seeds of heirloom tomatoes—is playing his or her special role in that mission.

Someone who has found his or her place in the grand scheme of things becomes a fountain of vitality and inspiration to others. Life grows through him or her even if he or she is unaware of it.

Most people have an innate desire to leave behind something that will outlive them. Having a legacy completes us. It is natural to want to be remembered long after our own time on earth has passed.

What happens when a person suddenly is besieged by a desire to die and to be forgotten? Suicidal thoughts may seem to be caused by various traumatic life experiences, but the true cause is more internal and spiritual. A person that wishes to die feels that life has been wasted on him or her.

Although we now understand the

physiological events that occur when a person succumbs to depression, the true cause of despair remains individual and obscure. Science can only observe it as it is happening in the body.

Psychologists can help a person investigate that depression by digging deep into the underlying psychological cause. Sometimes, however, years of psychotherapy won't help. The cause is not in the things that made that person sad.

Oftentimes despair is caused by the person's refusal to transcend events in the past and the present to see who he or she is despite them. When the individual is unclear of his or her role, unexpressed or even unrecognized passions become a destructive force in his or her life and the lives of others.

Despair is like being internally aimless: like Aladdin was before he unearthed the lamp.

It is about being so cut off from where your heart truly lies that you can no longer feel it or see where it wishes to take you. A true desire is like a beacon. If you cannot see it, you cannot move toward it and out of the place in your psyche that causes you pain. This pain is from a separation from the Self. And yet the passion to integrate is there—unable to escape and wreaking havoc inside you.

It is not always possible to know what your true desire is just by asking yourself. However, it is possible to observe yourself and what interests you. Interest is the unconscious gateway to the expression of your unique genius—the door to your true desires and life mission.

Each life-form performs a unique role in nature. A worm lives to soften the earth so that water will reach the depths of the dirt where a seed is hiding. It does not think about the seed that benefits from it. It thinks about its need to burrow beneath the ground.

We have desires that seem to have no reason for us. But they have a reason. Nature is designed this way. Each life-form on earth performs a function that serves another. Each individual person has a desire that may seem senseless in the context of that person or his or her family, but it is actually deeply essential to the improvement of the lives of others—people that person may not even know. Like the worm under the earth and its desire to obey its own nature of burrowing through soil, a person's passion is there for a reason that benefits the greater whole.

Uniting Passion with the Psyche

I have met someone whose life demonstrates what happens when a person's passion is derailed. I will call her Anna, although that is not her real name. As a young woman, Anna was instinctively drawn to the myth of Cupid and Psyche—the myth about the marriage of the conscious mind and the body's passions. She read it every night before bed and talked about it constantly.

Cupid, or "Eros" to the Greeks, represents our instinctive passions; and Psyche, the conscious mind. It is the myth that lent its name to Psychology for the study of the human mind. The name Eros is related to the Akkadian word *ereshu*, which means "*to desire*" and, more importantly, "to request."[6]

Anna did not know this, of course. But

---

[6] Edenics.net, s.v. "eros," 2009-2010 http://www.edenics.net/english-word-origins. aspx?word=EROS.

she read it constantly as if her life depended on it. It seemed that even if she didn't know how her life would turn out in adulthood, she unconsciously knew that the lessons that she was tasked to learn were in that story that fascinated her so much.

Anna was very beautiful. Her face bore the resemblance of Greek statues. A proud aquiline nose and full red lips accentuated her large dark eyes. Although her mother admired her for how she looked, her mother was disapproving of her interests.

As a child, her daemon urged her to perform behavioral experiments on the pet cat and her younger sisters. She would tie a short string to the cat's tail and put an anchovy in the end. The cat would go around in circles for hours until Anna's mother discovered it. Likewise, her sisters would find themselves surprised that they had given up their favorite dessert voluntarily because of Anna's mind games. She was not doing it to be mean; she was a natural behavioral scientist in need of guidance. Her mother, however, did not understand the source of her disturbing interests. Anna was constantly reprimanded for what her mother thought were bullying behaviors, but she was constantly praised for her physical attractiveness. As a result, she became so increasingly dependent on her looks for approval that she lost sight of what interested her most—psychology.

The young woman unconsciously chased her mother's vision of how to make use of her good looks to gain approval. She detested travelling because she suffered from an ear imbalance, but she agreed to work as a flight attendant at a time when they were chosen mainly for how they looked. She had wanted to get an advanced degree in psychology but decided to forego that to please her mother. It occurred to her that she could work in the day and study at night. Instead, she did what her mother suggested: focus on a job she really thought was beneath her. The choice made her an extension of her mother's passion for travel and no longer her own person. Through her, her mother pursued a dream that she could no longer fulfill in her own life.

The pursuit of another person's dream is never a good idea, and it could rob anyone of the motivation needed to be successful in that enterprise. Anna could not sustain it, of course, and ended up feigning headaches to get off work in order to spend time with a boy she did not really love. She got pregnant out of wedlock early in her twenties and had more children later on. The care of her children prevented her from pursuing anything else while they were young.

On the outside, Anna seemed fine. She could laugh with friends and seemed to enjoy good food. Inside, however, she had deteriorated so much psychologically that she could not sustain any job. She gained sixty pounds and would sleep constantly, leaving her children in front of the television for most of the day. She lost her looks and yet was still addicted to things that she could wear or makeup she could put on in order to make herself beautiful again.

The people around her who didn't understand what was going on would say that she was lazy. But this was not true. It was not laziness and lack of concern for her children that was immobilizing her. She was in despair. Her daemon generated fears that detracted her from completely squandering her internal resources on another person's agenda.

Unable to return to the part of herself that knew what course to take or which direction to go, she progressively increased her dependence on her mother, for she was the one who had ideas on what to do next. She also ironically blamed her mother for how her life turned out. In truth, her mother was acting only out of a desire to help Anna, for she believed her daughter to be lost. But as *The Name* reveals, because her mother saw her as lost, so she was.

I do not blame her mother. It was Anna that allowed her mother's opinion of her to drown her own internal voices. She chose to be her mother's creation instead of being a creator in her own right as she was intended to be. In a way, she played out the dilemma of Psyche in the myth of Cupid and Psyche. Anna's lack of trust in her own Cupid, the metaphor for her inborn passions, had wounded it and left her spiritually impoverished. Her mind told her to ignore the inner stirrings of her soul to keep her mother's approval, because she had learned that her interests were not acceptable.

Her despair was telling her that the life she had chosen was not what she was alive for. It was the daemon going on strike. Her Cupid had gone back to Olympus where only the gods (the powerful) can reside, and her Psyche must toil in obedience to Aphrodite's conditions to get him back. Olympus symbolizes creative heights and the actualization of potential.

Aphrodite represents the attainment of beauty and love—more specifically, self-love—for she is depicted carrying a mirror and gazing at her face. Born emerging from a shell, with pearls at her feet, Aphrodite's birth symbolizes transcendence from pain and tears.

Simply put, Anna had been tasked by her own self-love to search for her own passions. She had forgotten to seek her own approval of herself. She was not fulfilling her sacred purpose to serve the cause of Life by pursuing what interested her most.

She reported being taunted by a dark demon in her dreams. She even gave it a name that was curiously the name of an ancient god of healing, demonized by latter religions. She didn't know it, of course. But her subconscious latched on to that name. Her unconscious mind was sending her an urgent message that she was repressing her path to healing.

The daemon—the rejected passion—had become a threatening presence in her mind. Her unconscious was trying to communicate to her conscious mind about internal events that she needed to become aware of. It was using the only language it knows: archetypal symbols. The daemon continued to torment her until she finally took the time to understand the stirrings of her own soul. It was not until she took notice that she had failed to fulfill her own calling that the demonic force in her dreams began to appear as the benevolent image of the Virgin Mary. "A great evil is trying to get into your house. Pray, pray for protection," the Mary in her dreams had said.

At first she believed it was a warning of an intruder trying to get in her actual house.

But later on, she realized that in her psyche the Virgin Mary represented the "Holy Mother"—the one that served to purify her, versus the image of her actual mother in her psyche—the one that led her astray. In this instance, the "great evil" was the alien desire of her real mother that was occupying her internal house, asserting its residence, and claiming her internal resources.

A few days after that, she called her old best friend from school after avoiding her for years. They began reminiscing over a cup of coffee about their friendship. Her friend had recounted ordinary events that happened when they were in school.

When she returned home, it was as if she regained a part of her soul that had been lost in the choices she made. She began rummaging through old things and found her old school books and started rereading them. Months later, she surprised everybody when she enrolled in graduate school to study Family Psychology.

Although she did not end up finishing her degree because of the cost, the fact that she enrolled asserted that she was getting her life back. Some classes in a master's degree program qualified her to teach English in a specialized school for children with disabilities.

For the first time, she stayed in one job and with one employer longer than a year— even if her mother disapproved. She slowly lost weight and began attending to her children more.

Seeing her friend had reminded her of her old passions. Although she did not become a psychologist, her aptitude for understanding behaviors gave her a unique approach in teaching English as a second language to the language impaired. Because she remembered who she is, she could look forward to the future and dare to dream again. Those rekindled dreams were her beacon out of the darkness that had dimmed her passion for her own life.

Anna's life taught me that the daemon ignored will sabotage any course of action that takes us away from our cause. It threatens to bring us madness in order for us to work harder at finding our way back.

If we do not heed the call of our inner passions, it is as if we are suppressing what is bursting from us, keeping it trapped within until we implode.

When you heed the daemon's call, it unleashes a vitality in you that is inexhaustible. What you give out feeds you inside. Giving becomes an act of receiving.

I think this is how we were designed to live. We are all meant to be self-generating energy sources. But to be that requires courage, for those you love will not always understand.

Your purpose is etched in what you enjoy and what you find interesting. Joseph Campbell, the author of *The Hero with a Thousand Faces* had a powerful way of saying it: "Follow your Bliss." Indeed, if you spend most of your life doing something that does not interest you in any way, your daemons—the unconscious powers that dwell in you and the guardians of your sacred purpose—will engineer a takeover, and your body will go on strike. Your body will refuse to move or give you joy until you do what you were made to do.

Finding what interests you is difficult when you have learned to view it as a threat, a waste of time, or a wild animal you must tame. It does not always present itself as something that is obviously financially rewarding or socially acceptable until you take the effort to understand it. That tension produces ingenuity.

When you receive a call to do something,

you must heed that call even if it does not make any sense at the beginning. It will make sense if you take that journey. Investigate it. If you don't have the money to go to Alaska, for example, and you've been curious about it for a long time, at least read about it. Read everything about it. Any beginning is a beginning. This is not about what is logical but about what will give you back your interest in your own life. Attempt to live in complete faith that your passions, however irrational, serve a function that is essential not just to you but to others as well. Make a space for it amidst the chaos of your life and allow it to be your sanctuary. The part of you that is happy must have a home in time and space—even if it is only in a notebook or for five minutes of your life.

If it will save your body and quiet the demons that keep you immobilized, then why not do it? Do it in progressive allowances. First, allow yourself to think about it. Then, allow yourself to enjoy thinking about it. Give it space and time, and that space and time will grow.

If you do not know what your passions are, gaze at the demon—the symbol for the thoughts that torment you—for it is your daemon in disguise. What that means is this: you must strive to decode the fears that keep you chained to your uncomfortable psychic position and find in them clues to your inner path and the barriers you have put before you. These barriers were there to protect you in the past, but now all they do is hinder your own growth.

Invert the hole and turn it into the mountain it was meant to be. For example, if you lament not having a home, first, define what a home is for you. What makes a home? Whatever answer you come up with will be your own contribution to The Answer to That Question. Create this home. Draw it, write about it, and talk about it. Use whatever space and resources you have. Bright ideas grow from a combination of challenges and desires. The Brooklyn Bridge was made of such things.

Sometimes, the demons will continue to come masked in their terrifying, distorted form until the extent of one's purpose has been fulfilled. Sometimes, they never really leave, because you have not completely understood the force that is pulsating within you—what its true purpose is.

It is when you continue to flee the void in your soul that the call for your creative power remains a demonic force in your psyche. Despair is your resounding call for urgent self-knowledge. It is, in fact, the siren of your true calling. It is saying: "Leave the underworld! Be courageous and gather your dead. Trust in the path toward the light and do not look back, for that is the only way to revive them!"

Do you wish for kind people in your life?

Be that kind person. Your soul seeks for what you can give. You seek kindness because that kindness is in you, and you know what is needed for kindness and why it is important. Find a soul that needs that kindness and be that person's saint. You can be the fulfillment of your own unfulfilled needs if you learn to embrace others as part of your larger Self.

The Patron Saint of Darkness

Mother Teresa was a Catholic nun who founded the Missionaries of Charity in Calcutta, India, in 1948.[7]

Her daemon drove her to work in one of the most depressed and impoverished parts of the world to seek out the poorest of the poor. It was here that she generated hope to those who were hopeless. We later found out that the depression of the environment in which she chose to fulfill her missionary work mirrored the one gnawing within her.

It was in Calcutta that she externally alleviated the suffering she could not permanently alleviate within. It generated in her the capacity for extraordinary compassion.

While the world turned their faces away from the unspeakably destitute, she braved this

---

[7] David Van Biema, "Mother Teresa, The Life and Works of a Modern Saint," *Time*, Special Edition Reissue 2012, 30.

suffering and salved it with whatever emotional and physical resources she had. Her heroic mission caught the attention of the world. She became *Time* magazine's cover story on living saints and later received a Nobel Peace Prize for her humanitarian efforts. Her words revealed that it had not been easy to commit to her calling, but that doing so expanded her desire to give more

. "I have found the paradox that if I love until it hurts, then there is no hurt, but only more love."

By going beyond the reaches of human comfort to bring hope to those who needed it most, Mother Teresa inspired many others to do the same.

But there is something about Mother Teresa that is more than just a linear success story. Ten years after she died, a book entitled *Mother Teresa: Come Be My Light*, based on her own private writings and letters, revealed that she suffered from chronic depression when she began her missionary work. The Catholic world was surprised to find the living saint who spoke of joy doing God's work was suffering from a desperate despair. How she persisted in her solidarity with the destitute despite her illness makes me wonder; usually a depressed person can't even have the motivation to bathe.

However she managed, she later on expanded the reaches of her ministry to other parts of the world. It seemed later on, that she finally had embraced the darkness as part of what motivated her. To a theologian priest named Joseph Neuner,[8] she wrote: "I have come to love the darkness. If I ever become a saint, I will surely be one of 'darkness.' I will continually be absent from heaven—to [light] the light of those in darkness on earth."

In the wake of this revelation, many

---

[8] David Van Biema, "Mother Teresa, The Life and Works of a Modern Saint," *Time*, Special Edition Reissue 2012, 30.

questioned the authenticity of her faith. Neuner believed that her darkness helped her in her mission. Perhaps because she knew the despair that those she helped suffered first hand, her compassion was authentic. It was a driving force that helped her persist in the extraordinary difficult missionary work she had done.

Mother Teresa died in 1997. The former U.N. Secretary-General Javier Pérez de Cuéllar said: "She is the United Nations. She is peace in the world." It is like as it is the heavens. The black holes generate the cluster of light that animates the galaxies.

Perhaps it is not easy to digest or even believe that if you find courage to immerse yourself in the darkest darkness in order to uncover the light there, you yourself can become the source of an immense light.

Chapter Two

—ɷ—

Despair as the Canvas for Calling

"The sadness will last forever."

—Vincent Van Gogh's final words

I was around nine when I first heard the song "Vincent" by Don McLean. I didn't know anything about Van Gogh or his story at the time, but the song moved me to tears. The guitar that plucked the notes one by one soothed me as if it were a lullaby. I asked my father about it, and he told me the sad story of an impoverished European artist who cut off his own ear and then painted himself before he took his own life.

I thought it was strange that someone would write a song about a person who was obviously out of his mind. I, of course, changed my mind nine years later when I saw his paintings in an art theory class that was part of my degree in Fine Arts. I found in the song a new layer of meaning, for I myself had learned to use the paintbrush to express something inside me that I could not capture with words:

> *"Paint your palette blue and grey,*
>
> *Look out on a summer's day,*
>
> *With eyes that know the darkness*
>
> *In my soul."*

Don McLean sang *Vincent* (*Starry Starry Night)*: to express a personal realization that was inspired by Van Gogh's famous work:

> *"Now I think I know,*
>
> *What you're trying to say to me.*
>
> *How you suffered for your sanity,*

How you tried to set them free.

They did not listen, they did not know how.

Perhaps they'll listen now."

The words of Don McLean's song lingered in my thoughts even if I didn't know exactly what they meant then. It was a puzzle that stayed with me until I sang it one day to my father. My father often asked me to sing when he visited me; it was a tradition we had since I was a little girl. As the words rang from my vocal chords, tears fell from his eyes and then, much to my surprise, even mine. I guess I never knew that my father knew of this darkness until then. I felt a compassion for him I never did before. He was a complex man. The song was about a beautiful darkness, for it was a cry to be understood. It was a lament for beauty that was continuously ignored and unseen.

Don McLean's song was a masterpiece about a masterpiece. Van Gogh made a portrait of his soul that connected to another artist using another medium centuries after he had died. At that moment, these two artists connected my father and I as two human beings—sharing a universal sentiment untainted by the trappings of our familial roles.

Van Gogh died at thirty-seven. Historians believe that he suffered from aggravated manic depression. In his manic phases, he would write to his brother Theo constantly. The letters he wrote revealed the artist's unique and inspiring inner life. He spoke of a stirring of something within him that had a higher purpose, although his conscious mind could not find the words to describe it.

When he moved to Arles, he made the famous painting that inspired the song. *The Starry Night* portrays the night sky as a dynamic movement of lights. He once said: "I don't know anything with certainty, but seeing the stars makes me dream."

The stars were his internal marker of beauty and peace. They revived him and replenished his internal resources. This was what motivated him to come out at night and paint more.

Vincent Van Gogh's spiritual elation to the beauty that he saw in the night sky did not save his life, however. When the elation left him, he was emptied once again. The emptiness motivated him to paint again and again in his manic phases, perhaps to recapture the spiritual joy he felt when painting. It was as if his daemon did not allow him to do anything else.

I have met a couple of people suffering from manic depression who tell me that although they abhor the depressive phase, they seem reluctant to heal, because they secretly look forward to the opposite phase when they are highly productive and creative. Productivity and creativity are the makeup of our natural state. They fear that once the depression is gone, it takes the mania with it.

I once said to a woman suffering from manic depression that it seemed to me that the depression is also a kind of manic sadness. "It's all manic." I said, and we were both silent for a while—wondering if that were true.

Why does manic depression go to opposite extremes? What is the psyche trying to do?

When anything wobbles to extremes it is usually trying to find a point of balance. A top only spins steadily when it has found its center of gravity. Manic depression may be the mind's way of searching for its lost center. The extremes are exaggerations of a natural phenomenon. Opposing forces tug at each other constantly in nature and within us. Think of opposable thumbs, the left and the right brain, and the Republicans and the Democrats.

We alternate wakefulness and sleep. This is how we consume our experiences and digest them in our unconscious. They are codified in the unconscious and spewed out as ideas and creative insights when we wake up. A pregnant woman's belly expands as the baby grows inside her and contracts when it is time to bring that baby out into the world, crying, desperate to return to its obsolete womb. It is just how things naturally flow through us. It is how we generate energy—how we create.

Manic depression to me, is the natural ebb and tide of emotions that are felt in an extreme way. The volume is somehow louder and more unbearable. The expansion and contraction is more violent than with the average person. Perhaps this is because the person suffering from it is birthing something bigger. The sphere that the spirit of that person spins on is larger; therefore, requires more energy.

Many people suffering from manic depression are highly creative to begin with. In fact, recent studies confirm the correlation between genius and mental illness. An article in a special issue about genius in *Scientific American* exposes the direct link. In the article, Dean Keith Simonton quotes the Greek philosopher Aristotle to highlight this point: "Those who have become eminent in philosophy, politics, poetry, and the arts have all had tendencies toward melancholia."[9] The article makes its case as true for many luminaries including Vincent van Gogh, Virginia Woolf, and even Galileo——who they say was "...was often bedridden with depression."

Perhaps this is how consciousness sometimes releases its vast quantities of creative energy. Mortals usually suffer the intent of the divine. We don't have the godlike perspective

---

[9] Dean Keith Simonton, "The Science of Genius," Scientific American, November-December 2012, 38, www.scientificamerican.com/mind.

to see the gigantic purpose that is coursing through us. So we drown in the moment—oblivious to eternity's grand design.

Creative geniuses often experience a sort of divine spiritual elation. It is as if they glimpse something so perfect and so transcendent it seems simple. But, the human consciousness cannot hold on to it.

It is very difficult to retain that spiritual elation. Mother Teresa craved it all her life after first hearing it in her head as the words "carry me into the holes of the poor."[10] She interpreted this calling as the voice of Jesus. The powerful inspiration that prompted her to adopt a radical life change created a larger void in her soul when it passed.

Witnessing absolute order and beauty can fill us so much that when it passes it leaves

---

[10] David Van Biema, "Mother Teresa, The Life and Works of a Modern Saint," *Time*, Special Edition Reissue 2012, 24.

a gigantic void inside—like a great love lost.

The emptying, however, is a signal that the inspiration has been swallowed by the unconscious, and it is time to generate specific sets of action. The process of understanding how to do this requires a kind of spiritual shutting down. It often feels like being submerged in darkness.

When you have no way of looking at that anguish from a transcendent perspective, you can be convinced that the suffering is evil, and it is going to taunt you for as long as you live. You would not appreciate that the dip into the abyss is the spring that will generate new heights of creativity. Acceptance leads to temperance. When you know why you are in that darkness, that darkness becomes a womb instead of a dungeon.

Great talent is usually accompanied by alternating feelings of grandeur and anxiety expanding and contracting in the psyche. It is a cue that the soul is birthing something from that individual. It is the higher Self that is hungry to see itself born into the world. That hunger is an invitation to find joy—not from food or relaxation but from being in harmony within. It is joy from knowing what you must do to be alive inside. What you do to alleviate your pain, whether you are successful or not, oftentimes helps others too.

The manic-depressive is using his entire internal cave to swallow his emotions in order to create otherworldly motivation, because inborn motivation has greatly diminished. What is the shape of that cave? Is it the shape of a mountain? Must you climb one to experience the inverse of your depths? Is it finding hope in the most hopeless place? Is it seeing bright stars in the darkness of night? What is the size of that canvas? What can you paint on it? The truth is, the only escape from feeling trapped in darkness is to first recognize that you are not trapped. You plunged into it willingly in order to find your core. So, do it. Swim in those dark waters and search for that lost but beautiful unrealized self.

It is the act of searching that creates movement and generates light. Sometimes acknowledging that you have no desire to move is movement enough. It already is an action toward self-definition. Once you know your starting point, then you can traverse slowly out of stupor, progressively into the question: "Why? Why don't I want to move?" The answer is the first spark of light into the journey out of darkness and into realization. The path you took from the point where you knew what you didn't know becomes a trail—a trail for others to follow if they choose to.

The work always starts from within. When the work within is complete, the world begins to mirror this transformation.

The task that is awaiting the person in despair is to understand the nature of the darkness that overcame him or her. It is a force of the soul, a calling that is yet to be fathomed.

At the moment of being submerged into the abyss of the soul, you cannot ascertain your place in relation to the whole. You cannot know what lies in front of you or behind you. Because you cannot see the whole picture and where you are in relation to it, you cannot move with deliberate purpose.

The manic stages begin when a promise of certainty is found in the pit of the unknown. The manic hungrily pursues the direction only to find that the path leads him or her back to where he or she was, and nothing has changed. Then, he or she crashes back into despair. But something changes in each rotation from darkness to light. The problem is that we tend to look outside for signs of change, when we should be looking within.

Van Gogh found calm in the way he saw the world around him. He perceived a kind of rhyme and reason in the ordinary rooms and ordinary people, in the flowers, and in the stars. It is by observing the world and finding beauty in it, as it is, that his cup was filled.

"I wish they would only take me as I am," Van Gogh once said. He saw the order of things as they were and was saddened by how alone he felt in this perspective.

Pioneers are always alone. They are the first drops of water that cause the first ripples on the lake before the waterfall cascades.

Without Van Gogh's depression and without his desire to hold on to the fleeting moments of joy when he painted, he would not have created his masterpieces. If he saw parallels between his artistic perspective and his emotional needs, he would have seen that his true desires were filled by the very act of expressing those desires.

I know that I am asking you to accept something that may be difficult to accept: that without Van Gogh's despair, he would not be the painter that he was. For how can something that destroyed him be the source of such inspired and transformative creativity?

Shiva looks to the Sky

In Hinduism, destruction and creation are attributed to the same god, Lord Shiva. The Dance of Shiva represents destruction, birth, and rebirth. Shiva rules over unity. He is depicted to have many faces: four facing the four directions, and one facing the sky.

This means that what is perceived to be five different experiences is actually just one thing—consciousness doing its dance of creation and destruction in linear time. In truth, the five faces are always present within us.

The Eye of Shiva located at his forehead represents foresight. Many people associate this with psychic abilities. The Eye of Shiva represents being aware that consciousness comes in cycles of destruction and creation. Because of this awareness, the enlightened soul will be able to foretell the future, he or she will become a visionary.

The Eye of Shiva is symbolic of foresight. A person in the throes of manic depression is unable to rise above the nagging of past and present sorrows and cannot see beyond them. When we see that we too, like the earth, come in cycles of night and day and winter and spring, then a sense of stability and calm will overlap the rhythmic changes that course through us.

I have learned to observe that prior to a great breakthrough, I experience an internal breakdown. By reminding myself that my anguish is the birthing of a new understanding, I am able to speed up the coming of my new and improved consciousness. My discomfort in the position I am in and why I am there become clues that something inside me has changed and it is time to reflect that change through my choices.

It is important that I am unable to reach out for those fillers that numb me. I take the time to look into that pain and decipher it.

When I can't, I just move and see where my feet will lead me. Then, it reveals itself.

When I become an observer of the feeling of mania or depression instead of its mere participant, I move from drowning in those waters to becoming the captain of my own ship.

In order to make sense of the transformation happening within me, I draw them, I write them down, or I find them in my surroundings and capture them in photographs. Then when I'm done, I gaze at what my emotions made my hands do and my eyes see. I begin to understand them and learn from them. What we create is always a self-portrait—even if we are photographing or writing about others. We only see the world through ourselves.

Vincent Van Gogh reached out for his paints to understand himself. In this way, he was able to demonstrate to himself that when one observes the beauty of the ordinary, it really does become beautiful—even the experience of sadness.

"The sadness will last forever,"[11] are perhaps his most poignant words. They are both tragic and triumphant.

The portraits of his sadness and his desire to be accepted for his simplicity did live on. If he hadn't shot himself (if he did), what would have become of him after he saw that the world had begun to see itself through his eyes? Perhaps Van Gogh was never meant to change. He was, however, meant to change us. Mortals suffer the intent of the divine.

---

[11] Michael Douma, curator, *Letters from Theo van Gogh to Elisabeth van Gogh,* Theo van Gogh. Written 5 August 1890 in Paris. Translated by Robert Harrison, edited by Robert Harrison, URL: http://webexhibits.org/vangogh/letter/21/etc-Theo-Lies.htm.

Virginia's Gift

Van Gogh was like Virginia Woolf in that it was at the aftermath of his death that his transformative influence grew stronger. Virginia Woolf was born at a time when women did not have the convenience of having the opportunity to be anything other than a wife or a mother. I say this as though it is no longer a problem. But when I read Virginia Woolf's famous essay, "A Room of One's Own," it still resonated.

She wrote:

"All I could do was to offer you an opinion upon one minor point—a woman must have money and a room of her own if she is to write fiction; and that, as you will see, leaves the great problem of the true nature of woman and the true nature of fiction unsolved. I have shirked the duty of coming to a conclusion upon these two questions— women and fiction remain, so far as I am concerned, unsolved problems."

The staggering honesty of her words penetrated the lie that I tell myself every day: that I am as free as my husband to pursue my passion. My husband tells himself the same thing. In truth, I am not. My love for my family is my shackle. Because I am a woman, I am by design destined to put my child first and to need the love and approval of my husband, it seems, more than he does mine. Men seem to be happy doing what they do first before they can welcome their family in. By choosing to be a wife, I have followed my husband wherever his dream has called him, abandoning plans I had nurtured since childhood. I did not have to. But if I wanted to have a child with a father to grow up with, what choice did I really have?

It seems that the dreams I allow myself to dream now are those that keep me by their side. By choosing to be a mother, I am split into three. Two-thirds of me now belong to my daughter and my husband. Whatever passion I have left in me for my own pursuit must occupy the time and space that my family does not need from me. The rest are spent attending to varying levels and types of housekeeping. I usually do not allow myself to mourn this loss of self, because I find fulfillment as a woman being a mother and a wife. It is precious to me. But the aspect of me that is not just a woman—the part of me that is a human being—is silently mortified. Life asks too much of women! I have to give more than I can, because more is simply needed from me.

While it is horrible to admit at some level that I begrudge my husband and my daughter for needing me to be there or to be "theirs" constantly, I am freed somewhat from the burden of it when I am able to see that it is not just my secret problem. The validation I felt reading Virginia Woolf's essay allowed a little more of me that is neither wife nor mother to live on. Through her words, I am able to accept what I suffer in silence as a part of being human. Someone else feels as I do! The suffering then becomes a gateway to a connection to someone who lived at another time and place. I felt compassion for Virginia Woolf and believed that because she was bold about her sentiments, I was given permission to accept mine and no longer be secretly tormented by them. In that way, I feel less alone and strangely in the right place. Authentic expression of personal truths has the power to do that. It forgives us our frailties.

Even mourning over things we cannot change becomes a seed of that change. It elevates individual lives to the universal experience of life! It transforms misery into meaning and provides a gateway to acceptance. Life becomes grand, with all the bittersweet paradoxes it presents.

On March 28, 1941, Virginia Woolf drowned herself in a river near her home. She left a note to her husband Leonard that said:

"Dearest,

I feel certain I am going mad again...And I shan't recover this time...I am doing what seems the best thing to do.... I can't fight any longer...Everything has gone from me but the certainty of your goodness. I can't go on spoiling your life any longer...I don't think two people could have been happier than we have been.

V." [12]

Like Vincent Van Gogh, who may have felt that his destructive cycles made him a burden to his bother Theo, Virginia Woolf believed herself and her suffering to be an inconvenience to her husband, Leonard. It is ironic that what she expressed as an unsolved problem of women in the literary world helped transform it. We realize that women should

---

[12] The British Library Manuscript Collections Diaries, 1930-1931 (microfilm)

have the same capacity as men do to think and share those thoughts eloquently on paper. Her work is important to the development of modern feminism. It gave women material to fight for equal rights in the 1960s, around twenty years after she died. Her words became the immortal voice of a subjugated woman's cry for change.

Her suicide letter reveals that while she was intelligent and had a point of view that was ahead of her time, she did not have the resources we do today to understand her depression. She called it mere madness. Had she seen her "madness" as a boiling desire for change unrecognized, she may have chosen to use the pen, not the river, to exorcise her demons.

Virginia Woolf's authentic desires transformed her worldview violently and constantly. It was the source of her genius. She tried to remain the same because it was expected of her or perhaps because that was the extent of change that was possible at the time. That was what was driving her mad. She did not know what was happening to her and feared it.

Woolf felt that the world was better off without her. But even her brief stay made an indelible mark in the history of literature. Because she did not understand the desire that was driving her to question her worth, she distrusted it and sought to destroy it by destroying herself. Struggling against despair only deepens the darkness. A way to overcome it, I find, is to see it as an empty cup—a cup that must be filled by your own self-knowledge. Gather that substance first and then let it flow. Then the cup will become a pipe. Whatever you release from that pipe invites more in.

It is very frightening for most people to gaze at what is stirring within them. I often observe people suffering from depression struggle to manage their thoughts—pushing them deeper into their psyche so they don't have to deal with them. But the forces of what we truly want will run their course whether we look at them or not. The subconscious, where the desire is pushed, is ill equipped for sound judgment and will express these contained desires out into the world however it can. Then, you will find yourself living out your passions in their lower forms: as addictions or neurotic obsessions.

The act of making sense of it and why it is there generates awareness. It peels another layer of darkness—of the unrecognized. It generates light.

Chapter Three

—ᗰ—

Recovering Real Life from Fiction

"Of course it is happening inside your head, Harry, but why on earth should that mean that it is not real?"

—J. K. Rowling

Everybody knows J. K. Rowling, the author who made the world's youth read again in the age of Internet and computer games.

The famous author of the Harry Potter series had admitted going through depression prior to the release of her first book. She had been quoted to speak of it in a way that parallels a dementor's attack. A dementor is a vile fictional creature in the Harry Potter series that sucks out joy from a wizard or a witch. But

I recognized the dementors when I read about them. They were there that night in Bangkok when I looked down at the elephant seven stories below me and wished to drop myself beside it.

Of J. K. Rowling's own despair she said in an interview for the London Times in June 2000,

"Depression is the most unpleasant thing I have ever experienced...It is that absence of being able to envisage that you will ever be cheerful again. The absence of hope. That very deadened feeling, which is so very different from feeling sad. Sad hurts, but it's a healthy feeling. It is a necessary thing to feel. Depression is very different."

On page eighty-five of *Harry Potter and the Prisoner of Azkaban*, Ron, one of the main characters, said this upon an encounter with a dementor: "'It felt weird,' said Ron, shifting his shoulders uncomfortably, 'Like I'll never be cheerful again.'"

Many parts of her book series seemed to have been inspired from the experience of struggling with debilitating despair. In fact, the name of the shadowy villain, Voldemort, translates to "flight to death." Voldemort's name seems to signify a death wish. Does Harry Potter stand for that tiny voice of hope inside us that hangs on and continues to seek joy?

There were many breakthroughs peppered within the books that resonated with me because they seemed like the same breakthroughs I made while making sense of the despair I experienced when I was in Bangkok.

J. K. Rowling's fiction depicted a battle with the overwhelming shadows of the desire to die and the temptation to believe that the darkness should be feared. She also managed to show how to overcome it.

The dementor sucks out a wizard's happiness until he feels that he can no longer feel happiness again. To drive this illusion away, a wizard must cast a spell: the Patronus charm. The spell creates a bright light that comes from a wand; it is generated by a powerful happy thought. It usually takes the form of an animal specific to the wizard. It reminds me of native American animal totems that are actually spirit guides which help an initiate attain self-awareness.

The charm's name seems to have been derived from the Latin word *patre* which means "father." Perhaps because it not only shields but aggressively drives away the darkness, it is like the protective love of a father.

There are powerful memories that give our lives meaning if we allow ourselves to see them that way. They can serve as a kind of Patronus charm against the tormenting thoughts that come with despair. It does not have to involve other people loving us or a moment where we have achieved something worthwhile. Those things tend to lose their flavor in time. I find that what works for me are memories of peace experienced alone. It may be the memory of seeing the rays of the sun pour out of the clouds while on a swing or of hearing classical music for the first time.

I remember walking to school one day from my mother's house and seeing a round tree that seemed like it was covered with white flowers. As I moved closer, the flowers seemed to be mysteriously jumping around the tree. I thought my eyes were deceiving me—but were the flowers fluttering? I was surprised to find that the flowers were not flowers at all, but thousands of butterflies feeding on smaller flowers of the same color blooming on the tree. I remember stopping in shock. It was like a painting—a moving painting. The sun's rays made the tree appear to glow. The morning carried with it a fresh grassy scent. And I was utterly alone in the street: the sole audience to that amazing sight. It was like a greeting of a goddess.

I was filled with so much awe that day. I felt fortunate to have witnessed something so unusually magical that it felt like I was touched somehow by the divine.

When I remember that day, I am able to gather the strength to believe that my life is worth something. I cannot explain why.

That day has served as my Patronus charm on many occasions. I only need to access the memory to remind myself of something that remains pure and untouched inside me. It has driven the weariness from my heart and has revived me from the drudgery of believing that the world is an ugly place and that I am a hopeless victim of my own failings.

What I saw was independent of anything

I had done. Nothing about it could be attributed to anything that I had to earn. It was just given to me, and I was unworthy of it. It would have gone unobserved had I not passed by that tree that particular time of day when the morning sun made the fertile tree glow. Because of that, I feel blessed.

Rowling portrays these powerful memories as a magical charm. And they can be that if you know how to access them at will. If you can wield them like a wand, they can save you from being swallowed by your own despair.

The metaphor has indeed captured the imagination of millions of readers. Mesmerized by the authenticity of her work, the world consumed Rowling's work like their lives depended on reading it. It carried with it an elixir—a profound truth masked in fantasy.

Rowling's Harry Potter became a mass

instruction on how darkness can be overcome. Most importantly, it dramatized how a person's genius can come from whatever it is that has cursed that person's life. It is in keeping with the tradition of great myths. It is Hera that initiates the heroes.

Successful fiction often is not fiction at all, but rich symbolisms for actual events in the author's unconscious. In most stories, as in the case of the Harry Potter series, the task of man is to take the journey of the hero, as Joseph Campbell puts it, to face his own darkness so that he becomes the light he seeks. Joseph Campbell, the father of mythology, unearthed a common theme in all myths. Expanding on Jung's discovery of archetypal symbols in dreams, Campbell says that myths are collective dreams.

Myths are more useful when they are not judged by their historical value. They are the histories of our internal world. The symbols in mythology uses the language of our dreams and visions. They are the way the breakthroughs of consciousness transcend time and pass on from individual to individual. They are like coded instructions for universal psychic events. The stories we create that use these mythic themes contain this language.

When a person goes through despair, that person has lost the ability to perceive himself as an entity that is part of this universal dance of consciousness. He or she has lost his place within himself amidst the forces of other people's noise. He or she is trapped in the unknown Self. This Self makes its introduction as a desire. That desire is the unrecognized power, lurking within, that is waiting to be expressed. It is the genie trapped in a lamp that is buried in a cave of forgotten treasures. Gems are symbolic of life lessons.

When a person is in despair, motivation to do anything seems to be inaccessible.

Motivation requires purpose. But that sense of purpose has to be authentic. You cannot force yourself to feel passion.

Many people strive to motivate themselves with things or labels. They toil endlessly only to find that they still feel empty inside. That is because most people cling to false identities: identities they borrowed from people they believed were successful. Their real purpose has for some reason been compromised. While false identities are not bad in themselves as they serve a valuable function in the psyche, they can be very damaging when the person no longer looks for his or her true identity because of them. A false identity is a narrative one tells himself or herself in the interim of recognizing the real one percolating underneath.

As a person develops a healthy acceptance of his true nature, adopted narratives dissolve, and the authentic story of that person emerges. His inborn cause and what he believes in become evident in his actions and choices. When the authentic is embraced and not judged through the lens of other people's eyes, that person's creative power is awakened.

False selves are usually first adopted to salve old psychic wounds inflicted during childhood—when a wider perspective is still unavailable to the consciousness. In time, we are supposed to shed them. Some people, however, cling to them tightly simply because they have nothing else to replace them with. I find that when people do this, they are sure to eventually suffer from varying levels of despair.

When a person has embraced the false self as his or her own, the individual will appear to forget the real one. But beneath the surface of that adopted self is the shape of his or her true power, trying to push away the false self that is keeping it from exposure. The real self then seeps out in distorted ways: either as an addiction or a perversion. It becomes a dark force that is sabotaging the fake life that grew around it. It cannot fully come out of hiding because a false identity is usurping its rightful place.

How can you find happiness when it is someone else's idea of happiness you are pursuing? How can you feel success when it is somebody else's standards you are measuring yourself against? It is like feeling your way through a dark room and looking for a light switch that has been covered with other people's clutter.

You suffer a pair of shoes that do not fit you. It is the suffering that is telling you that you need shoes that do not bite your toes and injure them. Shoes are meant to make walking easier, not harder. If you wear your own shoes, you are comfortable to walk your walk. A life that does not fit you is like bad shoes. You learn to live with them, but you can't really get anywhere significant with them on.

Depression can be relieved by medication. Medication convinces the pleasure receptors in your brain that you have found something that satisfies you (like food or sex). But your body will not secrete neurochemicals that give you a sense of peace on its own without true satisfaction. True satisfaction comes from the fulfillment of true desires. If you have drowned away those desires and replaced them with the noise of other people's measures of success, how can you ever hope to get what you truly want?

Rowling's work can be viewed as a symbolic map out of despair. Her hero bears the emblem of Zeus, the god that rules over creation. I see Harry Potter's thunderbolt scar on the forehead as a symbol for creative inspiration born out of surviving a great darkness. Rowling spoke in the subterranean language of symbols and provided a map into the magical world of empowerment. How do we find this magical identity, the thing that enables us to manifest anything from nothing but the will to do it? How do we uncover what lurks behind the cloak of our mundane and powerless lives?

Rowling's fiction is about the hidden world of power and the darkness that covers it. It is more real than the stories we tell ourselves every day to avoid reaching for a more meaningful life.

Rowling gave me a name for the power I found beneath my despair. I have psychic markers of things that truly make me feel glad to be alive (like the tree filled with thousands of feeding butterflies). I can drive away the thoughts that torment me into believing that my own life is worthless to me.

In the embrace of ordinary life, magic materializes. It changes the way we experience the world. For Rowling's Harry Potter, the certainty of what truly makes one happy cannot be corrupted or sucked away. That, and there's nothing a box of chocolates can't fix.

Harry Potter, it seems to me, was the biography of Rowling's inner world and how she overcame her own *Voldemort*—her own 'flight to death.' Rowling gave me a concrete map of the schematics of my inner power. I have within me, a psychic wand. It can protect me from believing that the darkness will not end. We have better luck generating our own light than searching for it in unknown places.

The butterflies on the trees are still in my mind even if I can no longer visit the tree. The image for some reason is where I have placed the portrait of my true self. It is the image of my eternal bliss. It is my Bodhi tree.

Darkness will always come. It is important to know how to allow the light to shine from us. It is sometimes just as simple as recognizing when we are happy and keeping the memory of that joy within our heart's reach.

One of the faces of Shiva looks to the sky, representing transcendence. While we are in the flow of destruction and creation, a part of us must remain above it. We must see beyond the chaos of our existence while being engaged in it.

A friend who is a professor of philosophy once told me that there is no such thing as chaos in a timescale. We only perceive it as chaos because we cannot see its totality. But all chaos organizes in time.

As I hover around the cycles of my own darkness and light, I move closer and closer toward the source. The dips of my being and the heights, my virtues and my vice, and my future and my past all emanate from one thing in me—the Larger Self, the one that pulsates within all of us. It is this that generates the strange unconscious passions that urge us to go there or do that. When things become confusing for me, I return to that certainty.

I am a single force radiating outward, and I am able to rise up from darkness from that single point of illumination. I am able to gaze at the darkness and see it for what it is. It is the new shape of what I am and what I am about to create.

Epilogue

—⚉—

It was during the conclusion of a yoga teacher training class that I felt the culmination of a spiritual journey to healing. My mentor, an American woman who lived in Prague, revealed that she had suffered from depression. Like me, she was an ordinary person. And yet, she had given me a valuable gift: the gem she unearthed from her own abyss of despair. It was in the form of these words from Mark Twain: "Forgiveness is the fragrance that the violet sheds on the heel that has crushed it."

My mentor's entire practice was about forgiveness. It was about forgiving our bodies for being unable to bend more than our ego demands. It was about forgiveness as a gateway to serenity. Through forgiveness, the measures of "who-is-better" dissolve into an honest practice of self-healing. Her entire workshop seemed to emanate from this core breakthrough.

In my study of the esoteric, perhaps the most important thing that I have learned is this: the body bears all the sins of the mind. When I use the word "sins," however, what I mean is more the transgressions of the psyche to its own well-being. This can range from a simple thing such as failing to apologize out of pride to more grand and ongoing offenses to the soul such as living a lie.

All those thoughts that we tortured ourselves with, the feelings we suppressed and repressed, and the love we wanted to share but instead withheld did not disappear when we chose to ignore them. The body becomes the receptacle and the prison of these rejected inner forces.

When we heal our bodies, we are actually performing an act of self-forgiveness. We set ourselves free. There can be no real healing of the mind when the body is not engaged in the process. That cup needs to be overturned; its contents, released. Sometimes, medicines are needed to remind the body how to heal when it has already forgotten. But the body knows how to heal itself.

The best healing of the mind, I believe, comes from the heat of body movement. I sometimes feel that I am burning away my old mind when I engage in an intense campaign of physical activity. My new movements seem to be creating a new mindset.

More and more research is showing that the mind and the body mirror each other. When we are fearful and wish to retract from our environment, our bodies stiffen and contract. When we wish to let go of our fears, our body expands and our muscles relax. We are able to access movements we never could before.

When we feel exposed and unprotected, we eat more than we should and, in time, become obese. When we feel brave, we shed that protective layer of fat and create muscles that give us actual physical strength—strength that supports our newfound bravery.

Then our bodies begin to look like our psychic habits. The mind in turn becomes bound by those habits, because the body has created itself in the image of our predominant thoughts. It is like a seed growing roots on the ground it fell into. Whatever nutrient it finds in the foundation it is planted on becomes the content of its fruit. The only way to force our minds to break away from plunging deeper into habits of thought that keep us in darkness is to muster enough will to turn our bodies into a source of light—a source of self-discovery.

The body must be moved in new ways in order to ignite new pathways inside our minds.

Just as the muscle that is ignored for a long time becomes cold and weak, neural networks that are not visited recede. The mind is no longer able to cross those mental bridges that can potentially show new avenues of thought. The segment of our psychic pathways comes to life again and ignites new sparks of inspiration when the body starts giving it new information. A vibrant creative life becomes possible when the intent to heal the mind meets the act of healing the body.

Yoga, I find, epitomizes this point. All yoga prepares us for the union of mind and body. The word "yoga" means "to unite."

Only the harmony of mind and body produces lasting peace—peace that is no longer dependent on the events outside of us but generated from within. Inner peace has no external cause; it is a decision we make.

One of my closest friends introduced me to this concept around fifteen years ago. He did it by highlighting to me the important role the body's condition plays in the behavior of the mind.

I was in my twenties when I first met him in an aikido dojo. I went there to follow an old crush from college and was not really interested in martial arts. While I ended up not seeing much of that boy, I was surprised to find that it became more important for me to practice aikido. I was not only drawn to how the movements felt like a dance but also to the philosophy the practice is founded on. It was in aikido that my young mind first experienced achieving peace through body movement. The practice of aikido can be as violent and as aggressive as any student makes it. But, if followed in the traditional way, it can be a spiritual practice in itself.

The founder of aikido, Moreihei Ueshiba, believed in non-resistance. He taught that the force that attacks you can be turned into a force that protects you if you learn to anticipate it, accept it, and wield it.

The goal of an aikido practitioner is to harmonize his or her movements to that of his or her opponent's so that the force of the attack can be diverted to restrain him or her. In aikido, it is the attacker that determines how hard he or she falls on the ground or how much pain he or she inflicts on himself or herself. The practitioner only needs to step out of the way of his or her path to self-destruction.

The movements of aikido reflect this philosophy of self-defense. Aikido is about allowing all energies to take their course—being mindful only of how you respond to it. You see it in the actual practice, and you feel it at work inside. When I move in the correct postures long enough, something happens to me. I go into what feels like a heightened state of meditation. It is like I am half awake and half in a trance. I do not have to think about what to do next. The body takes over and does the thinking for me. It leads me to fall safely, as if each muscle in my body conspires to protect me from the sudden jolt of gravity. It knows when to bend, when to fall, and when to stand again. I become responsive to the present moment: undeterred by the fear of future pain. All that I have learned during practice comes together in a rhythmic dance that is as instinctive as it is learned through careful study and hard work. I never knew that the body could bear so much information my conscious mind cannot even comprehend. It knows what's coming and is prepared to do the motion necessary to protect me. It is in the practice of Aikido that I recognized that my body is my ally.

After every aikido practice, I used to share meals with other aikido practitioners in a nearby Japanese restaurant. One of them had an odd way of describing the items on the menu. I progressively grew more interested in what he was saying at each meal and made sure I sat beside him or near him. He became a friend and teacher.

It was his belief that the food we eat affects our emotional balance. Despair and joy is triggered by the kind of energy we consume.

He told me that sugar was poison, that's why even germs cannot live in it. He wondered loudly whether it was time to eat Yin or Yang foods. It was a strange, yet fascinating, discipline.

Yin and Yang are forces of light and dark—the idea of the balance between Yin and Yang is at the center of Eastern philosophy. Darkness and Light are twins that work together.

On days when I feel emotionally vulnerable and sentimental, my friend from aikido blamed the amount of fruits I ate that morning, and my temper on too much meat. I didn't know then that this very eccentric character would later influence my appreciation of Eastern philosophy. While it is almost impossible for me (or anyone else I know) to eat the way he does, I have learned from him that the body must be treated like a temple. All that we do to our bodies becomes part of how we look, how we think and who we are.

The nature of the food we ingest infects the quality of our habits of choosing—it later on becomes our character; it makes us unbalanced or harmonious inside. Whatever we bring in to our system eventually leaks into the external world as our behaviors. These behaviors affect how we feel about ourselves and about the choices we make.

Simple sugar for instance, gives easy access to energy. It burns bright and then burns out. It does not last and takes more energy than it gives. Perhaps that is why sugar is addictive. You're always trying to reclaim the last high.

When the body becomes used to having immediate energy that does not last, I believe it is harder to make choices that require trust and patience. It becomes harder to delay gratification. Most things that are worthwhile in life involves trust and patience.

People who would choose an ice cream bar over a meal, for instance, would tend to give in to immediate gratification instead of holding out for something more rewarding in the end. While I admit to a weakness for the occasional sugar, I know that it is symbolic of my need for a quick fix. It goes beyond what it does to the waistline—which is already depressing in itself. Sugar gets us used to unstable energy that gives us quick highs and sudden drops and the biological panic to recover energy balance that follows.

On the other hand, if your diet consists mainly of animal protein, doesn't it make sense that you are telling your body that animal flesh is your source of energy? Wouldn't the body respond by creating hormones that make you aggressive in order to be able to kill for food? Wouldn't the body behave more readily in reflex—reflex that makes hunting for food more efficient, bypassing crucial mental processes that produces sound judgment, such as deliberating whether it is good to attack or not? These instincts percolate, and in the absence of real prey, where do we turn the aggression that our predominant food choices create?

The point is, the machine running beneath the brain accepts whatever we feed it as information for the conditions of its survival. It will crave the food that we have given it to eat to maintain itself. This is how it engineers the appropriate capabilities. If we have to kill our food, what kinds of neurochemicals become available to us on a daily basis in order to continue to receive sustenance? How does that affect our moods?

In the same way, when we eat more plant products, what behaviors become inspired by it? In order to have plant food, we need to have in us the ability to patiently nurture and grow something. Perhaps it inspires the ability to see details in our environment and the stronger urge to plan and wait. Farmers know patience and trust in the coming harvest.

I believe that food is more than just the nutrition it contains. The food that we eat is symbolic of the kind of energy we seek and operate on. We can influence our moods with our food choices.

The mind is like a rider; the body, its

horse. While the rider directs the horse, the horse will only obey the rider if the rider has learned to respect the powerful beast he or she is riding on. If you nurture the horse and recognize its needs and its power, it will trust you and take you wherever you wish to go. Torment it with toxins and starve it of nutrients and it will resist you and even try to immobilize you. What is needed to tame a horse is to first give it what it needs to survive.

It is not just about quenching our psychic thirsts but also providing for our bodily needs. The creature beneath our minds must be given the care it deserves. It could be as simple as a good meal or a good night's sleep.

It was during my yoga training in Prague that all these distant scattered aspects of my life organized into a personal clarity. I experienced first-hand that all those years of study to achieve spiritual transformation pale in comparison to finally being able to reach my toes by allowing my body to breathe and be itself. You can say that the moment my hand flattened against the floor right beside my feet was when I felt like I had finally allowed myself to learn to surrender completely to who I truly am.

As I was lying down in the "corpse pose," I felt as if the earth was cradling me, that my body was one with it. My mind was unburdened by its weight and it was free to fly. I saw that the people I'd met and the gems they had shared had become part of the ingredients of my own gem. A facet of that gem is this book. My personal treasure sparkles with the light received from others who were courageous enough to share their own.

We are all made in the likeness of the force that created us. I believe that. That belief is weighted on what I have learned about nature and the force that runs it. This force is a creative energy that began when light first exploded in the universe, repeating its dance in various scales, and forming matter when it slows down.

It has continued that process over and over, in varying levels of existence. It continues as our human emotions and as our thoughts. But the force churns in the same cycles of night and day. The force that created the cosmos is within us just as we are in it.

We are all creators—able to generate light from our very own darkness. The task is to let that light exude from us even if we will never see the extent of what that light was meant to touch and reveal for others.

People sometimes resent it when I say that I have found enlightenment. I understand why they would. I would be annoyed, too, if I met myself years ago. People often associate enlightenment with superiority. But enlightenment, the way I understand it, is simply this: unconditional self-acceptance. It has nothing to do with who is better or wiser. It has everything to do with making peace with myself, with the things I do and fail to do, and with the things I continue to struggle with. They're all part of who I am.

I can see that my darkness is the shell of my light. I must crack this shell. I must unravel its mystery. I have grown to accept that the unknowns are part of what would be known, even if it is not I who will know them. I must ask the question for the question is a path. I am a path. I am a path of that light because I yearn to see it. As I recognize what I do not know, I come to know myself a little bit more.

So I no longer let the darkness or the demons that lurk there defeat me. When darkness comes into my life, I say hello and ask for an introduction. Then, as I gaze into its face bravely, I unmask a new aspect of myself waiting to be born. It is a seed that is seeking to become a tree. Its source is unknown, but It wants to live in the world, and It has chosen me as Its path.

I have discovered that I am part of something immortal. We all are. I carry within me all the knowledge of life. It is urging me to pursue Its cause and answer Its questions through the drama of my own life. It is the collective unconscious pulsating with wisdom gathered throughout the ages. Every instinct and reflex I have were lessons hard won by those who came before me. And with that, I feel neither just human nor a god—but both. With this realization of the two ends of myself, I am able to say with certainty that one can always find light in the dark. For light is born there the moment we look at it.

124

About the Author

Cecilia Sanchez Beltran is an internationally published writer and photographer now based in New York. Her talk, entitled *Why We Believe in Myths*, in 2010 for TEDxEast, New York, explored the parallels of myths and the human brain functions.

Prior to living as an expatriate, moving from one country to another with her husband and child, she lived in Manila. She received her education in fine arts at the University of the Philippines and later pursued a career as a creative writer in advertising for a decade. It is here that she became curious about the nature of the "big idea" which led her to the work of Joseph Campbell.

Her experience in the idea business collided with her personal fascination for Eastern philosophy and mythology. It gave her a unique perspective on the source of these universal symbols that spontaneously emerge from the human psyche.

She has conducted workshops on creativity in Manila, Prague and in New York. She is a co-organizer of the Joseph Campbell Roundtable, The Third Eye Awakening Workshops and the organizer of The Storytellers of New York.

INDEX

A

abyss (also see emptiness)   71, 74, 106
addictions   46, 88, 100, 116
    sugar   116
aikido   111-115
Aladdin, Arabic story of (also see symbolism)   27-31, 39
animal   2, 53, 92
    animal proteins   117
animal totems   92
anxiety   71
Aphrodite 34, 48
Arabian Nights Entertainment, The   27
archetypal symbols (also see mind)   49, 98
Ares   34
Aristotle   69
Athena   34
aura   18
authenticity   31

B

bibinkas (Filipino rice pancakes)   18
Blue Fairy Book, The (Andrew Lang)   30
Book of Symbols, Reflections on Archetypal Images, The (Ronnberg, A. and Martin, K.)   31
body   2, 24, 39, 42, 53-54, 101, 107-111, 113, 115-118, 120
    nutrition and   115-118
      respecting sacredness of   115
body-mind connection (see mind-body)
boredom   4
brain   67, 101, 117
    pleasure receptors and   101
British Library Manuscript Collections Diaries, The   85
butterflies   93, 102-103

Made in the USA
Middletown, DE
04 July 2021